Nutter

The London Bus Theatre Company

www.londonbustheatre.co.uk

ISBN: 978-0-9552893-1-6

A CIP catalogue record for this book is available from
the British Library

Printed and bound in Great Britain by R.Booth Ltd,
Penryn, Cornwall

"The search is now on for our "nutter" to be the talisman for any student who needs them!"
Sue Gray, Sir James Smith's College, Camelford, Cornwall.

"A Year 8 student said to me "Thanks for organising that Miss, I really get what it's all about now."
Sarah Parsonson, The Appleton School, Benfleet, Essex.

"The children loved it. It was very poignant showing what could happen if you make the wrong choices."
Julie Gregory, Milton Hall Primary School, Southend-on-sea.

"admirable, and the results speak for themselves with, essentially, less crime around the town."
Luke Calcraft, KeyMed Ltd, Southend-on-sea.

"The performances have stimulated a great deal of discussion in teaching groups afterwards."
Gaynor Wilson, St Martin's School, Brentwood, Essex.

Nutter was first performed at Palace Theatre, Southend-on-sea, 27 June 2007 with the following cast:

MC:	Chris Turner
Charlie:	Pat Tolan
Charlton:	Dafydd Bates
Amber:	Rhian Hillier
PC 1480:	Ross Evins
Youth Offending Team:	Tony Curd
Guardian:	Katherine Austen
Director:	Chris Turner
Lighting:	Darren Wilson

"For all the nutters in the world"

NUTTER is a mix of verbatim drama, forum theatre, monologue, tableaux and improvisation. Playing time is approximately one hour. The police scenes are transcriptions from actual cases.

Like the Joker from Forum Theatre, MC freezes the action on stage. In Act two, it's at the director's discretion whether pauses include audience reaction. The actor playing MC may feel able to improvise appropriate responses but should never lose sight of the text. In any event, the real power of the play lies in it being on the side of the angels from the outset.

Chris Turner, The London Bus Theatre Company

Characters:

MC: Part master of ceremonies – part narrator

Charlton: Sixteen, dominant, intelligent, a bully

Amber: Fifteen, rough, energetic, insecure,
              Charlton's sidekick

Charlie: Fifteen, only child, living with his mum,
              bullied by Charlton and Amber

PC 1480:   Professional

YOT: Adult, friendly, experienced

Guardian: Under sufferance

*The stage has a table and three chairs. On the table
is a vase slim enough to be secreted up a girl's sleeve.
In the vase are plastic flowers. The police officer needs
a TV and dvd/ video player, a notebook and pen. The
video "evidence" can be shot on mobile phone and
easily converted to required formats. In Act two, when
the first scene is repeated, MC is positioned on stage
to be "invisible", rather like a boxing referee – only
being noticed when they pause the action and address
the audience.*

Act one, scene one

KITCHEN, CHARLIE'S HOUSE
(a table, three chairs, a vase and flowers)

MC: *(to audience)* Two thirds of the antisocial behaviour in your area is carried out by people under the age of nineteen. Nicking cars, smashing phone boxes, graffiti, drink and drugs. If we show you what will happen to you if you decide to go down that route, it means you make more educated choices, but we also want to show you that it's not only the people having their windows smashed, their mobile phones stolen, who suffer. It's also the people in those gangs. Nobody involved in antisocial behaviour leaves unscarred. *(exit)*

CHARLIE rushes through the back door and stops at the table, out of breath.

Behind him, CHARLTON appears at the window, followed by AMBER.

CHARLTON: *(through the window)* Charlie!

Charlie jumps. They head around to the back door. For a moment, Charlie's rooted to the spot - he's not pleased to see them – then he goes towards the door with the idea of locking it; but he gets there too late. Pause. Face off through the door.

CHARLTON: All right, Charlie?

Charlie steps aside as Charlton and Amber enter.

AMBER: All right?

CHARLIE: What you doin' here?

CHARLTON: Funny, I was gonna ask the exact same thing. *(pause)* Well? Didn't you hear us calling? *(he punches Charlie in the stomach).*

CHARLIE: *(winded)* Thing is, I'm busy. Got things to do and stuff. For my mum, innit.

CHARLTON: *(mock-polite)* Oh, sorry, did you want us to wait outside?

CHARLIE: Yeah. No - I mean … D'you want something to eat? I was gonna have some cereal or something. You want something?

AMBER: Yeah, what you got? I'm starvin'.

Charlton leans over and strikes a glancing blow to the back of Amber's head.

AMBER: Hey!

(he kisses her roughly)

CHARLTON: I'm only thinking of your arse. It's getting bigger. *(Slapping Amber's backside)*

AMBER: *(to Charlie)* What you smiling at?

She shoves Charlie in the chest.

AMBER: Hit me. Go on. Hit me.

CHARLIE: No. I don't want to hit you.

AMBER: Pussy.

CHARLTON: How about a drink?

CHARLIE: You mean alcoholic?

AMBER: Duh!

CHARLTON: Your mum's not in then? That how you get away with bunking off school?

CHARLIE: She'll be back from work any minute.

CHARLTON: How about your dad?

Charlie doesn't reply.

AMBER: He hasn't got a dad.

CHARLTON: See, I don't get it. Your mum's at work. Your dad's ... wherever, but he obviously isn't here. You haven't got any sisters or brothers. I don't get it. What're you doing here? Why aren't you hanging with your mates?

CHARLIE: Dunno. I've got a playstation.

(Amber scoffs)

CHARLTON: See, I thought we'd agreed we were gonna go and mess with the Paki, teach him a lesson. I thought that's what we'd agreed. Are you blowing me out?

CHARLIE: I ain't blowing you out. It's the washing up and stuff, innit. For my mum.

CHARLTON: You're boring me.

CHARLIE: I ain't blowing you out.

CHARLTON: Boring.

CHARLIE: It's -

CHARLTON: Boring.

AMBER: *(slowly pulling the petals off the flowers)* He bores me. He bores me not. He bores me. *(throws the flowers at Charlie)*

Charlie goes to retrieve the flowers but Charlton steps in and punches him in the stomach

CHARLTON: C'mon, Amber, let's leave mummy's boy to wait for his mummy.

AMBER: *(to Charlie)* Mummy's boy. *(sliding the vase up her sleeve)*

Charlton and Amber head towards the door.

CHARLIE: Okay.

CHARLTON and Amber stop.

CHARLIE: I wanna come with.

CHARLTON: *(to Amber)* I dunno. What d'you reckon? Should we let him?

Amber shrugs.

CHARLTON: See, if you wanna come along, you gotta do it. You gotta lift me a bottle of vodka, all right?

CHARLIE: Yeah.

CHARLTON: You better not blow me out again. A bottle of vodka, yeah?

CHARLIE: Okay.

CHARLTON: *(his arm around Charlie as they leave)* Are we gonna get pissed or what?

Exit

Act one, scene two

POLICE STATION
(a table, three chairs, a tv and video)

MC: *(to audience)* Those three find a supermarket called Asifs and steal a bottle of vodka, but Charlie is not a career criminal and is identified using CCTV footage taken inside the shop. He is apprehended and brought to the Police Station for questioning. This is his first offence. *(exit)*

PC1480: This interview is being recorded. We are at *(location)* Police Station. It is *[current date]* and it's *[current time]*. I am police constable 1480, stationed at *(location)*. I have with me two other people in the room. Charlie will you introduce yourself with your name and address, please.

CHARLIE: Charlie Evins, *[address]*

PC1480: Okay. With you is your guardian, your parents can't be here today. Would you introduce yourself, please.

GUARDIAN: *(irritated) [name, address]*

PC1480: Okay. Before we go any further, Charlie, I must caution you. You do not have to say anything, but it may harm your defence if you do not mention when questioned something which you later rely on in court. Anything you do say may be given in evidence. Right, we are here today to look in to the incident which happened at Asifs Supermarket, Southchurch Road, on *[date]* at *[time]*. Where were you at that time?

CHARLIE: Home.

PC1480: You were at home? Was anybody at home with you?

CHARLIE: *(quietly)* No.

PC 1480: So you were at home, on your own, no one can give you an alibi?

CHARLIE: *(shakes head)*

PC 1480: Okay. What if I was to say that I can prove that you were at Asifs Supermarket?

CHARLIE: Dunno.

PC 1480: Well, either you were or you weren't. Were you at Asifs Supermarket?

CHARLIE: No.

PC 1480: Okay. I have a piece of CCTV footage that was taken inside the shop. Will you look at the screen over there, please. *(footage plays)* Was that you in the store?

CHARLIE: *(quietly)* Yes.

PC 1480: Can you speak up nice and loud for the tape, please. Was that you in the store?

CHARLIE: *(louder)* Yes.

PC 1480: Who was with you?

CHARLIE: I don't know.

PC 1480: Okay. Let's start again. You were in the store?

CHARLIE: *(quietly)* Yes.

PC 1480: Okay. Please remember that nods can't be picked up on the tape. You need to answer the questions. Did you steal the vodka?

CHARLIE: Yes.

PC 1480: Why did you steal the vodka?

CHARLIE: I – I don't know.

PC 1480: There's got to be a reason. Did you go in there thinking that you wanted vodka or was that the first thing you could get hold of?

CHARLIE: They said they'd beat me up.

PC 1480: "They said they would beat you up." So you *were* with other people, as we can see on the tape.

CHARLIE: Yes.

PC 1480: Who were they?

CHARLIE: I can't. They'll beat me up. They'll get me.

PC 1480: I can help you Charlie, but you need to tell me what went on and who you were with. Nothing's going to happen to you, but I need you to help yourself and tell me who you were with and why you were doing it. So, who were you with?

GUARDIAN: *(exasperated)* Tell him!

CHARLIE: Charlton and Amber.

PC 1480: Do you know their second names?

CHARLIE: Charlton Manning. Amber Hilder.

PC 1480: Okay. And why did they make you do it? Or how did they make you do it?

CHARLIE: Said he'd hit me. Said this time he'd do some real damage.

PC 1480: So, they – came round to your house?

CHARLIE: Yeah.

PC 1480: Threatened you with violence?

CHARLIE: Yes.

PC 1480: Why didn't you run off before you got to the shop?

CHARLIE: Scared, 'spose.

PC 1480: But you understand what you did was wrong?

CHARLIE: *(nods)*

PC 1480: What about the graffiti on the window?

CHARLIE: I don't know.

PC 1480: And what about the abusive words that were shouted at the shopkeeper?

CHARLIE: That wasn't me. They just did all that stuff.

PC 1480: So that wasn't planned?

CHARLIE: I dunno.

PC 1480: So was stealing the vodka planned?

CHARLIE: Yes, that's what they told me to do.

PC 1480: So let's just recap. These two friends came to your house, they threatened you, they hit you, and you went to the store and stole the vodka.

CHARLIE: *(nods)*

PC 1480: Let the tape show the defendant is nodding. You didn't write any offensive words on the window? And you didn't shout anything?

CHARLIE: No.

PC 1480: Right. I will stop the interview there.

Exit

Act one, scene three

YOUTH OFFENDING TEAM
(a table, three chairs)

MC: *(to audience)* Because Charlie has admitted his part in his first offence, and because it's not murder, this is what is going to happen to him. He will be given something called a "reprimand" by a specially trained officer. He may then be invited to attend the Youth Offending Team – The Y.O.T.
The Y. O.T is a government agency that has been set up to try and prevent young people like Charlie from offending and reoffending. If he breaks the law again, he could be given a Final Warning which is like a criminal record for five years, or up until the age of eighteen, whichever is the longer. Worse than useless if you're at school and trying to find a job!
Amber has also been arrested for her part in the incident at Asifs Supermarket. As she had already been given a reprimand for a previous offence, she agrees to receive a Final Warning on this occasion and has been sent for an introductory meeting with a member of the Youth Offending Team. *(exit)*

YOT MEMBER: Hi, Amber. How're you feeling? You okay?

AMBER: *(shrugs)*

YOT MEMBER: Right, my name's *[name]*. I work with the Youth Offending Team. I work with young people who get involved in crime. How much have the police explained to you about the following process?

AMBER: *(shrugs)*

25

YOT MEMBER: Right. Well, if I start by telling you it's a voluntary programme, okay. You don't have to be here. *(Amber gets up to leave)* However, if you go out of here and reoffend, you *will* go to court. And they'll ask me if you complied and I'd have tell them that, no, you didn't and it'll work out as a harsher outcome for you. *(Amber sits down)* D'you want to start by telling me why you are in here?

AMBER: *(defiant)* I didn't no nothing, did I?

YOT MEMBER: Well, there must be a reason you're in here.

AMBER: No. I didn't do nothing. It was Charlie that took it.

YOT MEMBER: Okay. So, you're here for no reason?

AMBER: Yeah. Well, apparently I called her a name and that's a crime.

YOT MEMBER: What name was it?

AMBER: I just called her a 'minging paki' or something.

YOT MEMBER: Well, that *is* a crime, Charlotte. It's verbal abuse and it's racially aggravated. And the police take it very seriously.

AMBER: Well, I didn't hurt no one, did I?

YOT MEMBER: You didn't hurt anyone?

AMBER: No.

YOT MEMBER: How's that?

AMBER: Well, it's true, innit.

YOT MEMBER: So it wouldn't hurt you if I were to call you "an obnoxious little brat who's throwing her life down the toilet"?

AMBER: You can't say that!

YOT MEMBER: You're right. I can't say that. And I wouldn't say that, because it's hurtful and hostile, not because it isn't true. I know you lost your mother last year.

AMBER: *(no reply)*

YOT MEMBER: The woman you shouted abuse at, the woman you swore at, the woman you spat at, Amber, she was a mother too. How would you feel if someone did that to your mother?

AMBER: I wouldn't stand for it.

YOT MEMBER: No, you wouldn't. It isn't right, is it? It isn't right. So, how d'you think your mum would feel if she knew you were doing things like that, if she saw you in this position? How do you think she would feel if she could see you sitting in court with a bunch of strangers deciding what they're going to do next with your life, and none of it good?

AMBER: *(no reply)*

YOT MEMBER: I can sit here and I could talk to you for hours, Amber, but that's not going to work, is it? It's got to be a two-way thing. We're here to help you, Amber, but it's up to you. Are you going to talk to me? Do you want to turn your life around?

AMBER: Yes.

Exit

Act one, scene 4

POLICE STATION
(a table, three chairs)

MC: *(to audience)* Charlton has been arrested for an assault, whilst in custody checks reveal he was wanted for questioning regarding the incident at Asifs Supermarket. *(exit)*

PC 1480: We've completed the interview for the matter which you were arrested for originally, but there is another matter that I wish to talk to you about. But before we go any further I must arrest you on suspicion of criminal damage. I must again caution you that you do not have to say anything, but it may harm your defence if you do not mention now something which you later rely on in court. Anything you do say may be given in evidence. Do you understand?

CHARLTON: No comment.

PC 1480: I'm investigating a matter of theft from Asifs Supermarket on *[date]* at *[time]*. Where were you at that date and time?

CHARLTON: No comment.

PC 1480: Were you with Amber and Charlie?

CHARLTON: No comment.

PC 1480: I have to tell you that I have CCTV evidence that puts you in Southchurch Road at that time.

CHARLTON: No comment.

PC 1480: Will you tell me where you were at *[time]* on *[date]*?

CHARLTON: No comment.

PC 1480: I must give you an extra caution, Charlton. When a suspect who is interviewed after arrest fails or refuses to answer certain questions, or to answer them satisfactorily, after due warning, the court or jury may draw such inference as appears proper. This applies when the person has been identified and can be put in the place of the offence. Do you understand?

CHARLTON: No comment.

PC 1480: Do you want to tell me where you were at this time and place?

CHARLTON: No comment.

PC 1480: In that case, I am going to conclude the interview here. *(exit)*

MC enters

MC: *(to audience)* Having given what is called a 'no comment' interview, Charlton's case will now definitely go to court and there is a strong chance he will receive a custodial sentence, somewhere between three to six months at a Youth Detention Centre. Think about it. When the police caution you they say, "you don't have to say anything now, but if you turn up in court and say stuff in your defence that you didn't mention before, what is the court going to think? That you're lying.

Amber and Charlie enter

MC: *(to audience)* What we're going to do now is fast forward and find out what these three are doing a few years after they stole the vodka. *(exit)*

Act one, scene five

A FEW YEARS LATER – MONOLOGUES

CHARLIE: *(to audience)* Just bought my first car.
A Ford Focus, nearly new, silver. It's all right, innit. I'm
getting promoted. Well, not promoted exactly. They're
closing the office in town and one of us was laid off,
but I was kept on. Gonna have to commute now though.
That's why I got the car. It was either that or move.

Still living with my mum, o'course. You didn't think I'd
moved out, did ya? I'm only just twenty. Plus she's a
mate, my mum, and she needs taking care of. And it's
cheaper.

Yeah, so I was lucky all that trouble with the police and
everything came well before my GCSEs. Had time to
get down to work, two "A levels", thank you very much.
Got a job with one of them internet service providers,
in Tech support. Been there almost three years now.
Spend most of my time on the phone trying to figure
out how to set up a customer's machine so it'll connect
right, to the ISP. Plus other general stuff, like you know,
answering questions like 'can I get broadband?' and
'how much does this, that and the other option cost?'
It's all right, innit.

Keeping well clear of trouble too. I know some people
say I'm boring and square. But I like it and I'm doing
all right and that's the important thing, innit?

Sometimes wonder how the other two are getting on.
But not for long.

AMBER: *(to audience)* You'll never guess who I saw out front the other day. Nah, not Posh Spice, what'd she be doin' down a Ford dealers at the roundabout? Nah, it was Charlie. Yeah, Charlie. Didn't talk to him though. Could'a done, 'spose, just didn't. Think he bought himself a brand new Focus so he must be doing alright for himself.

I'm working on a K-reg Escort me'self. The garage said it's mine if I can get it running. Which I have. I had to rebuild the top end: that's basically take the head off, strip out old valves and stuff. And I port and flowed the head as well to put in bigger valves. Yeah, that's right, I'm a car mechanic, if you hadn't guessed. Girls can do it too, you know. Got my NVQ Motor Maintenance level 3 last year.

It's going good, innit. Meet loads of blokes. Most of 'em idiots. Nah, that's not true, some nice ones. Don't tell Liam though, drive him crazy. Second thoughts, tell him, keep him on his toes.

I told him what I done the other day. What happened with the police and that. He didn't say nothing for ages. Just sat and watched TV and wouldn't look at me, only I knew he weren't really watching. I weren't gonna say nothing either, but I couldn't stick it. So I goes, "Did you want I didn't tell you? That's the way I am, Liam. What you see is what you get." And he goes, "I didn't think you were like that." So I goes, "like what?" And he goes, "stupid." And I goes, "I'm not stupid." I wouldn't have cried, but he just put his arms around me and I couldn't help it. Then he said he loved me anyway.

We're moving in together next month.

CHARLTON: *(to audience)* New York. Las Vegas. California. The Grand Canyon, the Golden Gate Bridge. I'm never gonna get to see any of those places and I can't stop thinking about them. Went into a travel agent's the other day and came out with a Trailfinders brochure for North America. No use to me. The Americans won't let me in. Not now I've got myself a criminal record. Disneyland. I won't be able to take my kids to Disneyland either.

No, I haven't got any yet. I'm too busy with the business. Yeah, I've got my own business now. Car valeting. It was impossible getting a job with my record, so I had to employ myself, set up on my own. It's going pretty well. I've taken on two other lads. We work alongside a car wash off the London Road. I know what you're thinking, 'a bully for a boss', but believe it or not I'm quite a good boss.

I'm not going to talk about youth detention, if that's what you're waiting for. We're drawing a line under that one. Got out of there as fast as I could. Some real bullies in there. Yeah, that's where the real bullies are. Actually, there's a better word for them but there's ladies present, so … But if you wanna lose weight, I really recommend it. It's real simple. I lost twenty-three pounds in less than three months. You just line up for your food, sit down, and then some f… somebody comes along and takes it off you. I call it the Blood Group diet: you wanna eat, you've gotta shed some blood. So, no, there's no way I'm going back there.

I tell you what I'd really like to do. Self-drive through Bryce Canyon, Moab, Monument Valley. That would be cool.

If you go, don't send us a postcard.

Blackout

Act two, scene one

KITCHEN, CHARLIE'S HOUSE
(a table, three chairs, a vase and flowers)

MC: *(to audience)* We are going to run the first scene again. I'm going to jump in, pause the action, and ask questions. *(to offstage)* Same again please. *(assumes "invisible" position on stage away from action)*

CHARLIE rushes through the back door and stops at the table, out of breath.

Behind him, CHARLTON appears at the window, followed by AMBER.

CHARLTON: *(through the window)* Charlie!

Charlie jumps. They head around to the back door. For a moment, Charlie's rooted to the spot - he's not pleased to see them – then he goes towards the door with the idea of locking it; but he gets there too late. Pause. Face off through the door.

CHARLTON: All right, Charlie?

Charlie steps aside as Charlton and Amber enter.

AMBER: All right?

CHARLIE: What you doin' here?

CHARLTON: Funny, I was gonna ask the exact same thing. *(pause)* Well? Didn't you hear us calling? *(he punches Charlie in the stomach).*

CHARLIE: *(winded)* Thing is, I'm busy. Got things to do and stuff. For my mum, innit.

CHARLTON: *(mock-polite)* Oh, sorry, did you want us to wait outside?

CHARLIE: Yeah. No - I mean … D'you want something to eat? I was gonna have some cereal or something. You want something?

AMBER: Yeah, what you got? I'm starvin'.

Charlton leans over and strikes a glancing blow to the back of Amber's head.

AMBER: Hey!

He kisses her roughly.

CHARLTON: I'm only thinking of your arse. It's getting bigger. *(slapping Amber's backside)*

MC: *(to audience)* Okay. Pause. *(the actors freeze in tableaux)* Is anyone getting bullied here?

AMBER: *(rubs her backside)* Yeah, me and Charlie.

MC: Give me the types of abuse we have seen in the first thirty seconds.

CHARLIE: Physical. I'm getting beaten up.

MC: Yes.

AMBER: Emotional…verbal.

MC: *(to audience)* Yes. Girls, would you ever put up with some boy saying, "I don't like the way your figure is going…sort it out"? No, of course you shouldn't. Would you ever put up with other girls saying they didn't like your figure? No, of course you shouldn't. Boys, would you ever have a girl tell you to change your hairstyle? No, I didn't think so. Another type of abuse?

AMBER: Sexual?

MC: *(to audience)* Yes. If you touch someone in a way that they do not wish to be touched, in certain circumstances that could be construed as sexual assault. These days we have to be very careful about how we relate to each other physically. *(pointing to Charlton)* This guy here wants to control everything and everyone he sees. Has he got a right to do that? No, of course he hasn't. Why does this guy feel so small, that the only way he can make himself feel big is by making everybody else feel small?

AMBER: Maybe he's angry.

MC: About what?

AMBER: I dunno, family problems, got no friends, whatever.

MC: Yes, I'll buy that, so, he takes his anger out on other people.

CHARLIE: *(sarcastic)* Maybe he's getting bullied

MC: Yes, maybe his dad hits him every evening, so he goes out that day thinking, "I've got to be in charge at least once today, I know, I'll pick on Charlie, 'cos when I get home tonight, my dad is gonna be in charge"! We see big scary bully...nah... big scary bully is usually someone very upset or frightened about something. What did he want Charlie to steal?

AMBER: Vodka.

MC: What happens to some people when they drink alcohol?

CHARLTON: *(embarrassed)* They get violent

MC: Yes. *(to audience)* The police will tell you that there is a direct link between alcohol, aggression and crime. Where has Charlton got the idea that he can slap his girlfriend...that it's okay to hit a woman?

AMBER: From the TV?

MC: How?

AMBER: You know, computer games, rap videos with thirty-something blokes singing next to teenage girls in bikinis...sick or what? The way they disrespect women.

CHARLIE: From his mum and dad?

MC: Yes, maybe he's watched his dad hit his mum and he thinks, "Dad hits Mum…men hit women…my girlfriend's a woman…she's gonna get slapped a few times…get over it." Or, maybe he has watched his mum cry all the time and he thinks, "I am never going to do that to a woman." It can work both ways. *(to actors)* Carry on from there.
(the actors pick up the scene)

AMBER: *(to Charlie)* What you smiling at?

She shoves Charlie in the chest.

AMBER: Hit me. Go on. Hit me.

CHARLIE: No. I don't want to hit you.

AMBER: Pussy.

CHARLTON: How about a drink?

CHARLIE: You mean alcoholic?

AMBER: Duh!

CHARLTON: Your mum's not in then? That how you get away with bunking off school?

MC: *(to audience)* Pause, *(the actors freeze in tableaux)* Why is Charlie bunking off school?

CHARLIE: I'm getting bullied

MC: Yes…maybe…

AMBER: To help his mum?

41

MC: Possibly. What is the big reason for people bunking off school…to do with their schoolwork?

CHARLTON: They can't do it.

MC: *(to audience)* Yes. Most of us never find the courage to put up our hands in front of our mates and say, "excuse me, I can't read or write very well." It's much easier to pretend that you're a hard nut… nobody asks about your homework.
What could happen to Charlie if he is wandering around on his own during the day, and not in a safe place like school?

AMBER: He could get mugged by someone like Charlton.

MC: Yes, he could become the victim of crime. By the way, why couldn't Charlton become a rock star?

AMBER: Eh?

MC: Where do you eventually have to go if you want to be a rock star?

CHARLIE: America.

MC: Exactly. Get yourself a criminal record… you can forget about that. What could happen to Charlie's mum if he doesn't go to school?

CHARLIE: Get into trouble with the police an' that…

MC: *(to audience)* …is the right answer! *(to actors)* Carry on from there.
(the actors pick up the scene)

CHARLIE: She'll be back from work any minute.

CHARLTON: How about your dad?

Charlie doesn't reply.

AMBER: He hasn't got a dad.

CHARLTON: See, I don't get it. Your mum's at work. Your dad's ... wherever, but he obviously isn't here. You haven't got any sisters or brothers. I don't get it. What're you doing here? Why aren't you hanging with your mates?

CHARLIE: Dunno. I've got a playstation.

(Amber scoffs)

CHARLTON: See, I thought we'd agreed we were gonna go and mess with the Paki, teach him a lesson. I thought that's what we'd agreed. Are you blowing me out?

MC: *(to audience)* Pause, *(the actors freeze in tableaux)* If you understand nothing else today, please understand this. Any abuse based on race in this country is a criminal offence. You say the wrong thing, to the wrong person, at the wrong time…you can go straight to jail…and "race" in this country also means the Scots, Irish and Welsh… *(to actors)* carry on from there.
(the actors pick up the scene)

CHARLIE: I ain't blowing you out. It's the washing up and stuff, innit. For my mum.

CHARLTON: You're boring me.

CHARLIE: I ain't blowing you out.

CHARLTON: Boring.

CHARLIE: It's -

CHARLTON: Boring.

AMBER: *(slowly pulling the petals off the flowers)* He bores me. He bores me not. He bores me. *(throws the flowers at Charlie)*

Charlie goes to retrieve the flowers but Charlton steps in and punches him in the stomach

CHARLTON: C'mon, Amber, let's leave mummy's boy to wait for his mummy.

AMBER: *(to Charlie)* Mummy's boy. *(sliding the vase up her sleeve)*

Charlton and Amber head towards the door.

CHARLIE: Okay.

CHARLTON and Amber stop.

CHARLIE: I wanna come with.

MC: *(to audience)* Pause, *(the actors freeze in tableaux)* and this is the whole point of the last forty-five minutes. Charlie is not a career criminal. Why on earth does he agree to go with them and end up being arrested?

CHARLTON: *(embarrassed)* He's being bullied.

MC: *(to audience)* Whenever you see a gang, you're looking at one person in charge *(pointing to Charlton)* and a load of people like Charlie ever so slightly scared of what would happen to them if they were not in the gang. What is the first thing you lose when you get bullied?

AMBER: *(cheeky)* Your teeth.

CHARLIE: Your confidence?

MC: Yes Charlie, your confidence. When you start to think that you're rubbish, what can happen then?

AMBER: You get depressed…suicidal.

MC: Yes, approximately twenty people every year in this country kill themselves because they are being bullied at school. Charlie is getting bullied, who could he tell?

AMBER: His mum?

MC: Yes.

CHARLIE: At school…your teacher?

MC: *(to audience)* Put your hands up if you'd tell a teacher. *(usually, very few hands are raised)* Put your hands up if you wouldn't tell your teacher. *(usually, most hands are raised)* Why wouldn't you tell your teacher?

CHARLTON: You'd get beaten up the next day.

45

MC: *(to audience)* "I gotta respect that. It's your reality. I'm not a teacher… I can't come in and say, "tell your teachers kids – it's gonna be great." I know you know someone in this school who is getting bullied, they might not get beaten up everyday, but they're always having the mickey taken out of them. They're the butt of people's jokes, they're never included in things. They'll be someone this lunchtime hiding in your school…they'll be in the library at a computer – or in a classroom they think is safe, or they might even lock themselves in the toilet. If you know someone who is getting bullied… even if you can't stand that person… even if you know you could never be their friend… if you can't go and help them, you're a wimp… and not only that… you're boring… you're a boring wimp.

AMBER: Charlie, how come you haven't told anyone?

Charlie: I dunno…ashamed…I s'pose.

MC: *(to audience)* "If I was getting bullied in your school…this is what I would do. I'd somehow find the courage… and I can't promise I'd be brave enough … to say, "It's stopping now." I would take every break time, every lunchtime and go up to every person in the school, whether I knew them or not, younger or older, and say, "sorry, I know you don't know me… that person over there is giving me a really hard time. Thanks." You might have to go through sixty, seventy, eighty, a hundred people but eventually you will find one NUTTER, there is one nutcase in this school who has the moral strength, the strength of character to say "You're getting bullied? I'm not putting up with that." And they're never who you think they're going to be.

And when you find that one NUTTER who is scared of nobody and nothing… all the wimps will get on your team, they'll say, "I knew it was wrong, I just didn't think it had anything to do with me." That's when you go to your teachers, you go mob-handed. 'Cos the following day when you come into school, that one person will keep everyone on your side, 'cos that's how they're made. And that NUTTER has to be you *(choose random audience member to point at… they'll feel uncomfortable but keep eye contact and persevere).* It's not negotiable. They've been through fifty, sixty, seventy people to find you. What are you gonna do… let them down? And if it isn't you, you have to go home, you have to sort it out, you have to come back…and it *has* to be you. And when it is you – they will keep you in their hearts for the rest of their lives. They will carry you like a good luck charm, and when they think of you it will inspire them. It will be the greatest thing you ever do… bar none. And it has to be you *(to Amber)* and it has to be you *(to another audience member)* and you, and you. If it isn't you, why are you here? See, when I go up the supermarket I can't find a car park space that says "wimp". Have I made a point? *(to actors)* Carry on from there.
(the actors pick up the scene)

CHARLTON: *(to Amber)* I dunno. What d'you reckon? Should we let him?

(Amber shrugs)

CHARLTON: See, if you wanna come along, you gotta do it. You gotta lift me a bottle of vodka, all right?

CHARLIE: Yeah.

CHARLTON: You better not blow me out again. A bottle of vodka, yeah?

CHARLIE: Okay.

CHARLTON: *(his arm around Charlie as they leave)* Are we gonna get pissed or what?

MC: *(to audience)* Pause, *(the actors freeze in tableaux)* Alcohol. Two things you need to know about alcohol because you're all probably going to drink it at some point. Firstly, it's a depressant. If you drink enough of that stuff, you will become increasingly depressed. Secondly, it's an anaesthetic, it's a painkiller. If you drink enough of it they can cut your leg off and you won't feel it. That's why you see people bleeding from head wounds, still fighting the police because they can't feel the pain. So, if you have too many alcopops, fall over and hurt yourself, the doctors don't know how much painkiller to give you should you need stitching up, because you've already had a load with the booze! Anybody here think that it's clever to get so drunk that you end up hurting yourself?

AMBER: Yeah, that happened to me. *(to audience)* I started going to clubs when I was fifteen. A mate and I wait for the bus into town and down a bottle of Thunderbird, lethal stuff, just to get drunk as quickly as possible. We get into the club with our fake I.D and try to dance and flirt. I suppose we're playing such a dangerous game because anything could happen. If the wrong person takes advantage of us, if my drink is spiked I wouldn't know. I'm drunk. I've woken up in the morning and not remembered how I'd got home. Lost my door key and phone once. Mum went mad.

Another time the police had to take me home because I'd got really drunk outside the local shops. I was grounded for six months after that. I've always thought if I didn't get smashed with my mates they wouldn't want me in the gang. I'm now beginning to see most of those thoughts are just in my head, and you don't have to get drunk to keep your friends. When I drink I can get violent. Got thrown out of a club for hitting this girl once. That's when it happened. I must have got talking to this bloke outside and he said he'd walk me home. Being fifteen, I thought this was nice of him. He wanted to go through the park, which in the back of my mind I knew I shouldn't do. But I was drunk. He was older than me and seemed friendly. When we got in the park he started to kiss me and push me on the floor and was on top of me. I was so scared, he was a really heavy bloke. It was only because I heard some voices nearby that I think he got off me. He frightened the life out of me. I'd done all that to myself, the fight, getting thrown out, some bloke nearly raping me, all by getting drunk.

CHARLTON: Come on Amber.

AMBER: Nah, I'm going home.

Black out

NUTTER was inspired by a chance remark from a girl in one of our bullying workshops. She said that telling a teacher about the problem was never going to be an option for her. When we asked the rest of the class if anyone agreed …they all did. After that, every school we went to we asked the same question…and got the same response. The thousands of pupils we worked with were saying that there was nobody in schools to stop bullying, that the ramifications of "grassing" meant making the situation worse.
This was their reality.

When we see someone being bullied, we are not just watching somebody having a hard time, we are watching them slowly die. They can just about get out of bed in the morning, they can just about eat breakfast, go to school, eat lunch, go home again… but they're dead. They're a functioning dead person. Expecting them to defend themselves is unrealistic. So, our new approach focused on the silent majority, the people watching it happen, but doing nothing.

We believe that in every institution there will be a "nutter", someone with a higher purpose…nobility, if you like, who sees that the duty of the strong is to protect those more vulnerable. We hoped that NUTTER would reassure anyone suffering from bullying that it is worth trying to find that person. We also wanted to remind the "nutter" in the audience that they had a job to do, and that the price of their courage and integrity was eternal vigilance, but that the reward was universal respect.

If just one person in your school is being made to feel, or do something that they do not want to feel or do, then all of us are diminished…and if you're being bullied…remember…there are loads of us who care and are trying to do something about it.

The London Bus Theatre Company

The London Bus Theatre Company is one of the leading Theatre In Education groups in the United Kingdom and can offer schools and colleges drama workshops and dvd's/videos on issues such as bullying, drugs, antisocial behaviour and interview techniques.

The London Bus approach is unique. Based on Augusto Boal's Forum Theatre of the Oppressed and run by Bristol Old Vic trained workshop leaders, the formats feature total involvement from the students and find sensible solutions to problems collectively.

www.londonbustheatre.co.uk